Winter to Winter

a year of seasonal change in the
Monadnock foothills

Jack Kraichnan

Snow Brook Press, New Hampshire

Design and Sumi-e illustrations by Laurie MacMillan
Printed in the United States of America by R.C. Brayshaw & Co.

ISBN-13: 978-0-9769036-0-4

ISBN-10: 0-9769036-0-1

After breakfast, she
Sends me outside to harvest
Poems from the land

Introduction

"Winter to Winter" records the drama of seasonal change in New England through regular observations written as brief poems. The poems contain both what I observed and what I associated with those observations. I wrote most of the poems during a daily five-mile loop walk in the eastern foothills of New Hampshire's Mount Monadnock, in a landscape of field, woods and wetlands. I took this walk in all weather from mid-December 2002 to mid-December 2003. In our increasingly developed and engineered world, weather is one of the last forces of Nature left wild. Being out in it for a year was a gift.

This is a nature book. It is also a book of meditations inspired by the economy and elegance of haiku. While all of the poems have the 5 7 5 syllable meter of traditional haiku, I do not claim that they meet all of the requirements of true haiku poems. The important thing to me was having a structure within which to work. Writing in a structured form forced me to distil my thoughts. I was rigorously honest in recording what my senses actually perceived, and resisted altering reality even slightly to accommodate an easy turn of phrase. The reward for doing so was transcendence of my pre-conceptions into a more complete experience of what was really there.

I found that the seasons are not as clearly defined as I had thought. This is why the book's chapter divisions are shifted from the individual seasons to the transitions between them. In winter it snows, but it also rains and is warm. In spring the birds sing, but the next day it may be too cold to sing. Summer's abundance is overwhelming, but its resources diminish rapidly. Fall is extremely bright at times, then grey. Each season has a little of the other three hidden in it.

I offer this book to those who may be trapped inside too often.

- J.K., Dublin, NH, 2005

Winter to Spring

Winter to Spring

Clear December air
On my cheek like cold metal
Moon is almost full

Cresting snowy ridge
Sun fills woods with spreading light
Orange as wildfire

Slick with rain trees reach
Glistening eel-black fingers
Into pewter sky

Warm mist over ice
Rain falling on melting snow
Pine scent in thick air

Stream runs fast and clear
Almost cold enough to freeze
Around snowy rocks

White pines swaying now
Northeast wind is rising from a
Whisper to a yell

Driving snow becomes
Time-lapse tracks of golden stars
In flood light's broad beam

Encased in clear ice
Trees transform winter daylight
Into countless suns

Snowfields on mountain
Like white markings on the flanks
Of sleeping grey cat

On wind-swept white snow
Dark, fallen branches lie still
Calligrapher's strokes

Snowflakes veer and swirl
Schools of darting crystal fish
In a windy sea

Wide ribbon of snow
Sags side to side on thin branch
Balancing on edge

Blazing on the hearth
Logs warm us with past sunlight
That fell on green leaves

Curving over rock
Winter brook reveals green moss
Beside pure white snow

Winter morning light
Casts summer evening shadows
Cold and from the east

Golden morning light
Gives warm look to winter day
Cold enough to kill

Culling cold today
Molecular lethargy
Trying to still life

From building's cocoon
I watch the day pass, deprived
Of the smell of snow

Snow-covered fields
White on mountain's light blue flank
Whale's battle scars

Beneath snow and ice
In dark of pond's still water
Turtles are waiting

In my bright, warm house
I know that I am weaker
Than the winter birds

Thirty-four degrees
After weeks frozen deep; breathe
The sweet evening mist

January thaw
Stream runs under snow, urgent
As a boy's desire

With the first bold touch
Of the rising morning sun
Snowfield blushes pink

Roaring from the west
Cold-air freight train ran all night
Bringing winter back

Wading in deep snow
Grey split-rail fence gleams silver
As last light skims field

Cedar waxwing flock
Eating maroon crab apples
Above bright white snow

Facing winter sun
Blue jays perch with puffed feathers
Snowballs in a tree

Frilled ice skirts reach out
From smooth stones in winter brook
Like rippling snail feet

Under skin of snow
Stone wall curves up wind-swept hill
Spine of hungry cow

Fox tracks from when snow
Was new, now path of raised discs
Undercut by wind

Lone paw print, perfect
In icy field's wind-packed snow
Conjures coyote

Grey winter limbo
Clouded sun casts faint shadows
Dry beech leaves hang still

Mercessant beech leaves
Translucent in winter sun
Thin as onion skin

In the cold, firm snow
Rhythmic steps are making sounds
Of big cat purring

Bubbling under ice
Brook speaks with the same timbre
As dry logs tumbling

Mountain in snowstorm
Blends into grey sky, a face
Almost forgotten

Bobcat's silent steps
In yesterday's snowshoe tracks
Sharing space, not time

Stars after sunset
Are revealed like leaves' colors
When green fades in fall

Illuminating
Without warming, moonlight floods
Silent winter room

Thick, steady snowfall
Deepens with slow certainty
Of a rising tide

Bushes and saplings
Tangled in their shadows weave
Dark lines on bright snow

Gently tapped, spruce boughs
Spring free of snowy blanket
As if roused from sleep

Snow falls from spruce tree
With the same thumping cadence
As grouse's wing beats

Sharp laugh in bare trees
Pileated woodpecker
Calls in winter woods

Pileated ate
Leaving piles of wood he pecked
Under old beech tree

Grey as spider's silk
Coating of ice holds spruce boughs
Motionless in breeze

Reaching across path
Beech and hemlock branch tips touch
Joined by sparkling ice

After the ice storm
Gusts of wind fill forest with
Sounds of breaking glass

Fallen from white pines
Tufts of dark green needles lie
On snow's bright ice shell

Blown from laden trees
Puffs of dry snow move wraith-like
Through shafts of sunlight

Winter sun reveals
Lacy ghost of fallen leaf
In brook's clear water

Moss on dead beech trunk
Faces winter sun with greens
Lush as summer woods

Dry beech leaves quiver
In gentle breeze that carries
Chickadee's spring song

Thawed from brook ice, drop
Hesitates and then resumes
Its downstream journey

Swollen with March rain
Brook outgrows its winter coat
Flat ice now submerged

Mother-of-pearl field
Morning light reflects from shell
Of ice-covered snow

Soft and bloody pelt
Marks transfer of resources
On snow's trackless crust

Peeking above snow
Fence line waits for warmer days
To restore its height

Twig in icy brook
Armature for freezing spray
Modeling antler

Dappled with shadows
Snow matches camouflage
Worn by paper birch

Orange-peel snow crust
Textured by countless impacts
Of falling raindrops

Bounding grey bobcat
Flowing over snow bank like
Water over dam

Mouse tracks in fresh snow
Tiny highway divided
By central tail drag

In gusty March wind
Spruce boughs, used to winter, flail
With agitation

Woodland snow tide ebbs
Stumps and rocks re-emerge
Brook's voice grows stronger

Melting snow layers
Superimpose collections
Of winter debris

Delicate beech twig
Sinks slowly into snow's crust
Falling through crystal

Blanket of fresh snow
Re-discovered innocence
Temporarily

In sculptural curves
Packed snow remembers wind's path
Among grey boulders

Smooth-barked grey beech trunk
Lies on snow pack, dignified
As whale washed ashore

Beech's narrow buds
Extend from twigs still holding
Last year's tattered leaves

Striped maple buds
Redden on olive-green twigs
Above sinking snow

Acorn tops burrow
Into March snow melting deep
Cylindrical holes

Layers of brook ice
Separated by air form
Resonant chamber

Fractal ice fingers
Reach toward each other across
Swiftly flowing brook

Snow's crust relaxes
Under warm breath of March's
Mercurial winds

Days away from spring
Subsiding snow pack's cool breath
Hovers in grey woods

Wet, granular snow
Water and ice together
Part winter, part spring

Snowmelt rivulets
Meander over dirt road
Carrying sand grains

Late winter snowfall
Impermanent as icing
On eager child's cake

Like night animal
Caught in daylight, snow retreats
Quickly from March sun

Cerulean sky
Puffs of snow from hemlock boughs
Greet the morning wind

Standing in snowmelt
Bark reddish-brown in warm sun
Hemlocks wear dark boots

Over the high falls
Water plunges, revealed through
Lace of melting ice

Swollen with snowmelt
Brook stands over stone in wave
Thick as molten glass

Tousled, stubbly field
Emerges from underneath
Winter's snow blanket

Late winter air's touch
Soft reconciliation
Between old lovers

Mourning doves exchange
Soft, hollow calls like breaths blown
Across bottles' mouths

Turkey vulture glides
Riding breezes from the south
Over melting snow

Green as old copper
Lichen on bark fragment melts
Down through late March snow

Sinking late March snow
Holds each fallen leaf and twig
In a fitted case

Rows of icicles
Sharp as crocodile teeth hang
From old log in brook

Drops of clear water
Fall from melting ice counting
Seconds of spring day

Trickles of snowmelt
Merge with mountain brook and roar
Over mossy rocks

Seditious snowmelt
Encourages rotting log
To disorganize

Freed from melting snow
Miniature club moss forest
Shades a passing ant

Flashing tail whiter
Than melting snow, lissome deer
Bounds through spring forest

Melting snow retreats
Evenly as a ripple
From grey woodland stone

Carpet of spring snow
Grows patchy as the plumage
Of a molting bird

Small tattered remnant
Of winter's snow blanket lies
On bare field's north slope

Wet with melted snow
Carpet of beech and oak leaves
Quiets my footsteps

Curling as it dries
Fallen leaf pressed flat by snow
Rocks in sweet spring breeze

I grasp dry oak leaf
And find it soaked with warmth from
Bright pool of March sun

Gnarled tree root holds
Dry rock in its elbow's crook
Out of swift brook's reach

Water strider's feet
Dimple rotating surface
Of brook's quiet pool

Porcupine shuffles
Reluctantly away from
Snow-wet acorn meats

Robins in fresh snow
Feathers fluffed against March cold
Pick up dark wet leaves

Varnish of clear ice
Accentuates rock's colors
After late March storm

Rushing spring brook climbs
Curving bank of sloping rock
Like stream of racecars

Fresh white snow collects
On the tops of shelf fungi
Forming pointed caps

Crystal stalks of frost
Lift their brown dirt blossoms up
Above thin spring snow

Dusting of March snow
Lies on thin ice like powdered
Sugar on clear glass

Tapering upward
Like dipped candles, icicles
Hang low over brook

Under April rain
Thin snow sheet on fallen leaves
Turns to ragged lace

Drops of April rain
Hang from sapling's thinnest twigs
Beneath swollen buds

Single thick beech root
Wrinkled grey elephant trunk
Reaches down brook's bank

Shaggy yellow birch
Looks like dog about to shake
Wet fur free of rain

Cold grey winter air
Seeping into April woods
Holds sharp scent of snow

Falling from branches
Snow punches dots and thick lines
Into white carpet

Jagged hollow stump
Tiny ruined castle wall
On a snowy plain

Grey stone wall laid dry
Has mortar of wind-blown snow
And smooth cap of ice

April snow adorns
Beech sapling with cotton balls
Where its branchlets fork

Broad boughs bent with snow
Hemlocks stand like silent birds
Wings tucked close for warmth

My left cheek is warm
As I walk south through the snow
In bright April sun

Twig with red buds lies
On bare log soaked nearly black
By melting white snow

Diffused in grey sky
Silver sun's light casts neither
Brightness nor shadow

Green and grey lichens
Blend birch trunk with the rock face
Out of which it grows

Robin's liquid song
Flows through gentle evening air
And stops as night falls

Silently searching
Hawk carves slow circles in air
Above April field

Dark green hemlock bough
Shimmers silver with sun's touch
On its flat needles

Silver striations
Of dry stump among grey rocks
Catch bright morning light

From dry northern bank
I look across forest pond
To shaded spring snow

With changing focus
Reflected blue sky becomes
Stones in clear water

Liberated from
Crystal confinement, snowmelt
Cascades over rocks

Southerly breeze bears
Scents of warming juniper
And damp fallen leaves

Tall tree amplifies
Woodpecker's machine gun burst
Staccato attack

Ducks and wood frogs quack
On warm afternoon while snow
Hides in the shadows

Tan as old oak leaf
Wood frog crouches on black earth
By emerald moss

Velvet-skinned red eft
Slowly grasps brown oak leaf stem
With its orange toes

Seen from underneath
Outlines of raindrops show through
Translucent spring leaves

Drop of spring rain rests
Silver bead on clover leaf
Reflecting grey sky

Blue heron mates flap
Angular wings in tandem
Trailing their long legs

Horizon extends
As pale blue mountains emerge
From soft morning fog

Shiny black beetle
Hurries over brown oak leaves
And hides under stick

Quicker than a thought
The spider I am watching
Has seized a blackfly

Stands of tall white pine
Weave their sweet and tangy scent
Into soft spring air

Framed by the window
Mountain's sloping ridge behind
Leafless maple's buds

Furrowed green beech leaves
Emerge from scaly tan buds
With beards of white silk

Translucent pale green
White birch's new leaves are bright
Against the grey sky

Soft grey May morning
Serene as the gentleness
After making love

Unfurling from bud
Tiny wrinkled maple leaf
Newborn's open hand

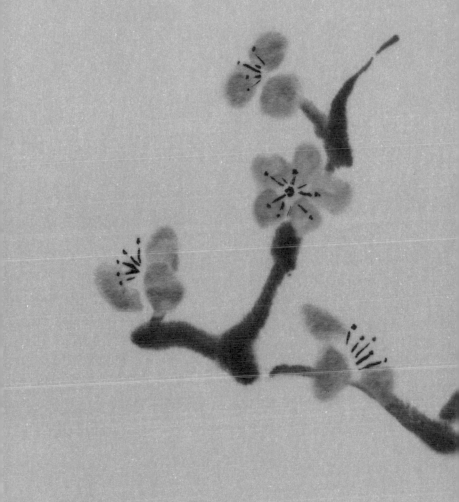

Spring to Summer

Spring to Summer

Whispering past trees
May rain strikes leaf carpet with
Popcorn percussion

Drops of May rain cling
To brilliant white garlands of
Hobblebush flowers

Newt pauses and hangs
Neither sinking nor rising
Beneath pond's surface

Glistening with rain
Red eft poses dragon-like
In forest of moss

Turning slate grey back
Robin becomes part of branch
In thickening fog

Evening silhouette
Woodcock rises spiraling
Into half moon sky

At lip of ravine
In warm, sun-dappled May woods
Rushing brook's cool breath

Water striders mate
Wandering the surface of
Clear woodland pool

Climbing Monadnock
We stepped where unknown footsteps
Had worn the rock smooth

Carved by the glacier
Smooth skinned grey rock elephants
Rest in mountain woods

Ethereal flute
Wood thrush amid tree's new leaves
After morning rain

Tom turkey poses
Bodybuilder with feathers
Powerfully flexed

Blades of grass support
Canopy of dewdrops strung
On transparent silk

As the ripples fade
Another raindrop falling
Above pond in May

Branching trunks in mist
Of pale greens and muted reds
Maples in new leaf

Striped maple holds
Limp new leaf pairs at twig tips
Like domed umbrellas

Sulfur butterfly
Pauses near darker yellow
Dandelion bloom

Against green hillside
Cherry blossoms appear mixed
With dandelions

Forest canopy
Closes softly as spring leaves
Unfurl completely

After the long rain
Wraiths of mist haunt the valley
Beneath sunset clouds

Serpentine wriggle
Of green ribbon tail propels
Newt through still water

One hind foot long lost
Red-spotted newt walks briskly
Orange tail whipping

Startled garter snake
Vanishes on forest floor
Scales hiss through dry leaves

Quick garter snake
Descends bank and swims through brook
With the same motion

Brook's flowing water
Reflecting sun's streaming light
Sparkle that stands still

Bubbles disappear
From clear brook water leaving
Base of waterfall

Painted trillium
Three white petals with red throats
Shaded beside brook

Red-backed vole scurries
Fluidly among grey stones
Beside forest pool

Mid-May sun's warmth soaks
Into green field; grasshoppers
Fly with rattling wings

Small black bee searches
Among bright sunburst petals
Of dandelion

Caterpillar-like
On reflected leaves, catkin
Floats in woodland pool

Yellow petals gone
Grey-headed dandelions
Give seeds to the wind

Tussling sparrows
Flit among rain-wet grasses
In May morning fog

Silent on strong wings
Goshawk flies into thick woods
Not a leaf disturbed

Green tiger beetle
Iridescent on grey stone
Takes wing with a flash

Iridescent green
Tiger beetle rushes to
Seize shiny black prey

Drinking from dew drop
Delicate thread-waisted wasp
Clings to blade of grass

Barely visible
Spider's thin web has trapped two
Green hemlock needles

Old leaves soft with rain
Only the crackle of twigs
Betrays my footsteps

Each step toward the brook
In woods quieted by rain
Makes its voice louder

In the morning mist
Clover flower's purple sphere
Holds clear water drops

Clover leaf shadows
Dance with gusting morning breeze
On southeast rock face

On this damp morning
Wisps of grey mist are blowing
Past the tall pine trees

In flat pewter light
Deep rose lady's slipper sways
Just before the rain

At the forest's edge
Two deer standing in sweet breeze
Vanish silently

A step from warm sun
Into cool leafy shadow
On the dappled trail

Rippling in the breeze
Tall grasses whisper softly
As the sky darkens

Yellow galaxies
Of long-stemmed hawkweed flowers
Float above green field

Speedy toad tumbles
Over rotting log beside
Motionless red eft

Black eyes rimmed with gold
Show potential leap within
Frog's ancient stillness

Soaked with fine brook spray
Fallen brown beech leaf adheres
Seamlessly to rock

Curling as it dries
A fallen maple leaf rests
Cradled by a fern

Rows of rounded clouds
With flat bottoms sit as if
On a sheet of glass

In the deep blue sky
Cotton ball clouds are moving
And shifting like thoughts

A cloud has switched off
The column of light that fell
On three green beech leaves

Gentle late spring breeze
Stirs soft-edged leaf shadows on
White birch's bright trunk

Bright in rain-wet woods
Pale green tips of hemlock boughs
Soft and newly grown

Through translucent sheet
Of thinned brook on wide flat rock
Dark green moss shimmers

In the pre-dawn rain
Robin's clear voice ripples through
Darkness and wet leaves

Indigo bunting
Blue so bright in the green field
That I do not breathe

In the morning field
Warm, moist air hangs motionless
Sweetened by clover

Dew drops reflecting
The clearing grey sky become
Brightly transparent

Gleaming damselfly
Metallic green with black wings
Beside the brown pond

From the blade of grass
Small brown butterfly has flown
To my fingertip

In dark morning woods
At green beech leaf's slender tip
Drop of last night's rain

Beech tree's smooth-barked trunk
Turned from grey to brown by rain
Glistens in dark woods

Heat of summer day
Sifts down through canopy
Of cool morning woods

Rustle in the trees
Of ocean waves retreating
Follows summer breeze

Bright orange mushrooms
Sprouting from a shaded log
Soaked black by long rain

Arching itself back
Small red eft can barely reach
Nibbled mushroom cap

As the daylight fades
Oak tree becomes silhouette
Cut out of the sky

Cloud of mosquitoes
Reminder that beneath thoughts
I am blood and bone

Field of tall grass rings
With cricket's shrill desire
In the summer heat

Fireflies in field
Conjure blinking cityscape
Out of soft night air

From the tangy heat
Of summer field I step
Into cool, sweet woods

With rustle of leaves
And heartbeat rhythm of hooves
White-tailed deer is gone

Swallow above field
Changes direction sharply
On quick, pointed wings

Alien voices –
Martians landing in the field?
No, they're bobolinks!

Early summer heat
Brook which rushed and charged in spring
Is growing lazy

On the wooded ridge
Gentle summer breeze blowing
Over soft green moss

Sitting on bright rock
I feel July sun's warmth
Above and below

Trace of truck's exhaust
In sweet air stirs memories
Of hitch-hike summers

Thick yellow pollen
Moving through purple clover
On a bee's hind legs

Spider's low web holds
Diamond raindrops in the sun
Just above the ground

Perching dragonfly
Perpendicular to blade
Of green summer grass

Dragonfly hovers
On glinting cellophane wings
Beyond the cliff's edge

Shadows of two leaves
Almost touch as summer breeze
Moves above smooth rock

Hand with nine fingers
Oak leaf on dry forest floor
Cupping bright water

Tall flowers near rock
Gathered in shadow bouquet
By low evening sun

In the windless woods
Leaves are motionless beneath
Ceiling of thrush song

After the fireworks
Fireflies continue flashing
In the tall grasses

Thunder before dawn
Voicing the cavernous growl
Of a dream tiger

Butterfly on rock
Opening its wings and then
Closing them again

Startled coyote
Charges up leafy hillside
With fluid power

With a hint of green
Bumblebee is not as bright
As yellow flower

Through the hot field's buzz
Thrush's clear song from near woods
Cooling as brief rain

Thinning July brook
Clinging to its lower bank
Flows around smooth stones

Shifting with the breeze
Shafts of light in forest pool
Turn brown beech leaves gold

In the mossy stump
Hidden fungus is revealed
By sudden mushrooms

Seedlings by old path
Fresh beech, oak and maple trees
Shorter than club moss

In the restless breeze
Dark green maple leaves showing
Their pale undersides

Rustling above me
Raindrops in the upper leaves
Before I feel them

Under thick grey sky
Smooth stones in the darkened brook
Blackly glistening

On the flat grey rock
Pool of morning rain reflects
Leaf's serrated edge

The sharp scent of pine
Cuts cleanly for a moment
Through thick July air

From the tall grasses
I am wet with morning rain
Already fallen

Fragments of old leaves
Lifted temporarily
On white mushroom's cap

In the shaded woods
Indian pipes' angled stalks
Disturbingly pale

Where tall white pines shade
Gravel road old needles hush
My crunching footsteps

The old rotten log
Has become almost as soft
As the forest floor

Under crisp blue sky
The goldenrod is turning
High-summer yellow

Curl of white birch bark
Bright in pool of summer sun
On the shaded path

On the sunny leaf
Beetle with odd shape has found
Partner of its kind

Around the boulder
Brook divides itself in two
And smoothly rejoins

In the thick stillness
Cicada's metallic buzz
Bobolinks are fledged

Field's orchestral buzz
Modulates as insects land
And take wing again

The distant mountains
Crisp and clear on drier days
Vanish in thick air

Eyes closed in deep woods
The August rain surrounds me
With a dome of sound

On the old stone bridge
Spider webs above the brook
Silvered by moist air

Small brown moth flitting
Among glistening grasses
In the August mist

Glistening mushroom
The purple of wampum shell
Rain has just ended

At rotting mushroom
Eleven newts have gathered
All of them bright orange

Where its flower was
Trillium holds one red fruit
Above treble leaves

Monarch butterfly
Tiger-colored velvet wings
Flitting past the oak

Summer to Autumn

Summer to Autumn

In still August woods
My ears strain to hear the songs
Of the silent birds

Mid-August morning
Oak tree is suddenly full
Of pale green warblers

After silent leap
Small wood frog is instantly
Observantly still

I try not to guess
Where next drop will fall in pool
From rain-wet beech leaves

With each step in field
Small grasshoppers are leaping
Unpredictably

Dragonfly squadron
Patrols crisp blue August sky
Above goldenrod

In the open field
Light summer rain is falling
Angling with each breeze

On fallen beech trunk
Old fungus at right angles
To those newly grown

Distant leaves have lost
Individuality
In thick August air

After so much rain
Forest is damp gallery
Of bright mushroom shapes

Mushrooms sprout in woods
And old road, cut by rain, holds
Pebbles on dirt stalks

Mushroom cap forms cup
As it's upper surface shrinks
In the drying woods

Pale yellow spider
Waits silently in tube made
Of silk-wrapped green leaf

Tractors mowing field
Are steadily approaching
Bee in tall thistle

August morning full
Of chickadees chattering
Like kids back at school

Fixing tumbled wall
Time flows in both directions
Stones lock into place

Sweet-smelling mown field
Ringing with sharp insect trills
Under wispy clouds

Seen between the trees
Forest floor beside mown field
Continues contours

Small spider crouches
Unmoving at the center
Of its spiral web

Elegant wood frog
Tan against tan faded leaves
Hidden in plain sight

Hobblebush berries
Yellow globes bright red on top
Once spring's white flowers

Green late August tree
Has dropped a single red leaf
Onto the old road

Grasshopper cleaning
Steps on each antenna and
Gently pulls it free

Caterpillar eats
Sides, then middle of grass blade
Methodically

Just above mown grass
Sulfur yellow butterfly
In late August wind

Red bodies coupled
How does dragonfly pair choose
Direction to fly?

Green mountain pierces
Dark September clouds hanging
Over foothill field

Thick September mist
Motionless in dark green woods
Quiet as sadness

Cool September rain
Clings to tips of hemlock boughs
Bright drops in grey woods

Sound wood at the core
Of rotting fallen hemlock
Trunk of tree when young

Deep red maple leaf
Fallen beside white birch log
Both now wet with rain

Shining in bright sun
Dark green oak leaves freshly washed
By yesterday's rain

Tiny drops of dew
Turn caterpillar's long hairs
Into pewter threads

Motionless lichen
Is dissolving ancient rock
Imperceptibly

Unseen cloud moving
Forest is suddenly full
Of light and shadow

By the shaded brook
Dark, wet scent of old mushrooms
Then dry leaves again

In the quiet woods
Cool sunlight and soft shadows
Dapple grey beech trunk

Beneath the beech tree
On smooth rock still cold from night
Butter-yellow leaf

On the forest floor
Colored maple leaves collect
Bright as summer days

The warmth of summer
Is gradually draining
Out of the forest

Moving in abrupt
Stroboscopic bursts of speed
Chipmunk circles tree

Tiny frog jumping
Lands on dry carpet of leaves
Sounding like raindrops

Bright yellow beech leaf
In its slow and silent fall
Tipping back and forth

Leaves that look alike
Show they have different shapes
In the ways they fall

Cold has nipped ferns brown
Now soft air from southern storm
Rustles colored leaves

Beside rotting log
Sapling gathers resources
Evens entropy

On the pool's surface
Fallen yellow beech leaves float
Held completely still

Water striders grouped
At center of shrinking pool
Shake reflected trees

Between oak's dark leaves
Fine white wisps of cotton clouds
In the dry blue sky

Autumn's shorter days
Thinning summer woods' dark green
With pale yellow wash

Glinting in the light
Of gentle September sun
Shiny black cricket

Crow in full voice flies
Approaching vanishing point
Of its raucous calls

Grey frost on green grass
I have not made ready yet
For the coming cold

Days after first frost
Breeze as soft as summer blows
Swaying brilliant trees

Thistle with brown stalk
Has one purple flower and
One of silver down

Through the yellow ferns
Sunlight reaches from behind
Maple leaf glows red

Moving steadily
Woolly-bear caterpillar
In the faded grass

Slope with autumn trees
Reflecting in black water
Of still beaver swamp

As light as her hair
On my arm the morning rain
Whispers on the roof

Tossing falling leaves
Brisk wind makes silver ripples
In thick dark green grass

Black with driving rain
Thick oak dances in strong wind
Casting off its leaves

Shallow forest pool
Reflects fragments of the sky
Between floating leaves

Colored leaves, of course!
But also tang in clear air
And my rustling steps

Browning autumn woods
Bright leaves like painted metal
Beginning to rust

Through cupping oak leaves
The early snowflakes falling
Drifting slowly down

Lighter than raindrops
Snowflakes falling steadily
Jiggle pool's surface

Leafless birch trees stand
Naked white among maples
Wearing finery

In the sudden rain
I stand under a maple's
Red-gold umbrella

Golden brown beech leaves
Translucently wet rustle
Softly in the breeze

Beside the pine tree
Among brown and withered ferns
Chalky-blue asters

Frosted with wet snow
Three tall maples in full leaf
Green, red and orange

Tips of green grass blades
Poking through fresh snow surround
Bright red maple leaf

New snow is crunching
Under my boots and summer
Seems a lifetime past

Not yet deeply cold
Melting through the early snow
Glistening grey rocks

Gusts of gentle breeze
Sweet-scented exhalations
Of warm autumn woods

Damp air grey and soft
As seaside summer melted
Early mountain snow

Autumn to Winter

Autumn to Winter

Maple leaves just down
I walk through leafy beech grove
In the golden time

Heavy rain has washed
Forest's bright colors away
Leaving golds and browns

Afternoon breeze stirs
Dry tissue-paper rustle
Of curling beech leaves

Sunlight and the calls
Of chickadees reach brightly
Through leafless branches

Drained into the brook
Heavy autumn rain cascades
Carrying large sticks

Puddle of raindrops
Held in fallen aspen leaf
Reflects an oak tree

In the leafless grove
I feel all the changing moods
Of the falling rain

Green grass at field's edge
Interspersed with strands of grey
Like my own whiskers

Thick ice fingers reach
Straight down toward the flowing brook
From clump of snagged leaves

Setting sun is bright
Only in some tall trees' crowns
As the woods darken

Patches of green moss
Are losing their resilience
Stiffening with frost

Pebbles in dirt road
Sunken by the frost like gems
Loose in their settings

In bare-tree forest
Oak leaves cover maple leaves
That fell earlier

In windless grey mist
Raindrops snap on flat brown leaves
Or join the swift brook

Only the beech trees
Are left holding leaves and those
Are like old paper

Cluster of mushrooms
Where the wind-blown beech trunk failed
Foretold its breaking

Over smooth grey rocks
Clear brook's steady flow contrasts
With my scattered thoughts

Through tall leafless trees
The low sun warm on my face
As I climb the slope

On the old birch log
Pale green moss so very bright
In November rain

In steady grey rain
Tall birch tree with no leaves left
Brilliant white washed clean

Two dry tree trunks rub
Hollow squeaking in grey air
That smells of winter

Uprooted pine tree
Holds a rock above the ground
Lifted by falling

Fresh snow in morning
My memory had not held
All of the brightness!

Under leafless trees
Dusting of bright snow reveals
The curves of the land

Soft day-old snow holds
The animals' steps preserved
As it will my own

Sunken in hard snow
Yesterday's boot tracks shelter
Dry wind-blown beech leaves

Old snow in the rain
Soaking up the falling drops
Sponge made of water

The cold brook rushes
Through fantastic structures made
Of its frozen spray

Day of greys and browns
Brighter now that I have found
Flock of chickadees

A moment of grace:
The winter sunset's colors
Not filtered by thought